Wheel around the world

Editor: Karen Adler
Designer: Sally Boothroyd
Teacher consultant: Ruth Crow
Production: Susan Mead

© Macdonald & Co (Publishers) Ltd 1983

First published in Great Britain in 1983 by
Macdonald & Co (Publishers) Ltd
London & Sydney

A member of BPCC plc
ISBN 0 356 09213 5

Printed and bound in Belgium by
Henri Proost, Turnhout

Macdonald & Co (Publishers) Ltd
Maxwell House, 74 Worship Street
London EC2

Wheel around the world

compiled by Chris Searle
illustrated by Katinka Kew

DOWNBY SCHOOL

Macdonald

Contents

Shout

Shout child, shout!
Stray from the beaten ways
And laugh out;
Sing and spring
While you can;
Can–can and dance and prance in the sun;
Son, shine and run;
Fly your voice,
Fly your kite,
Fly your life!

KEITH ARMSTRONG, *England*

11

Once the wind
said to the sea
I am sad
            And the sea said
Why
        And the wind said
Because I
am not blue like the sky
or like you

        So the sea said what's
so sad about that
                Lots
of things are blue
or red or other colours too
        but nothing
neither sea nor sky
can blow so strong
or sing so long as you

        And the *sea* looked sad
        So the wind said
Why

SHAKE KEANE, *St Vincent*

12

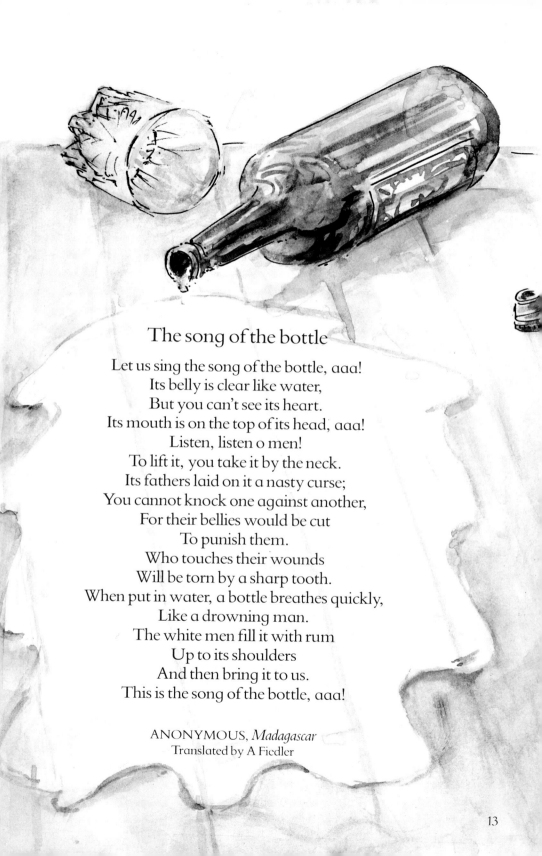

The song of the bottle

Let us sing the song of the bottle, aaa!
Its belly is clear like water,
But you can't see its heart.
Its mouth is on the top of its head, aaa!
Listen, listen o men!
To lift it, you take it by the neck.
Its fathers laid on it a nasty curse;
You cannot knock one against another,
For their bellies would be cut
To punish them.
Who touches their wounds
Will be torn by a sharp tooth.
When put in water, a bottle breathes quickly,
Like a drowning man.
The white men fill it with rum
Up to its shoulders
And then bring it to us.
This is the song of the bottle, aaa!

ANONYMOUS, *Madagascar*
Translated by A Fiedler

Some games we played

Thinking now of *Jacks and Ollies*
Cherry-Wabs there up the spout.
Let us have a game of *Golly* –
I'll touch you, then you'll be out.

Banny-Mugs and *Jumping Figures*
On the pavement by the door.
See how 'chalking out' just triggers
Shouts of wrath from Granny Gore.

I'll not go and get a message
When she asks me – no! I'll hide!
Peep around there from the passage –
'Way she shouts I can't abide!

Have you got your *Top and Whip* there?
I will let you have a go
Of my *Shuttle Cock and Bat,* where
You can lend me top, you know.

Aye! and *One-Two-Three-A-ler-ah* –
Auntie Sarah I did see,
Sitting on her bum-del-ler-ah –
Come and play a game with me!

NORAH HALLOWELL, *England*

Night

Silently sleeps the river.
The dark pines hold their peace.
The nightingale does not sing,
Or the corncrake screech.

Night. Silence enfolds.
Only the brook murmurs,
And the brilliant moon turns
Everything to silver.

Silver the river,
And the rivulets.
Silver the grass
Of the fertile steppes.

Night. Silence enfolds.
All sleeps in Nature
And the brilliant moon
Turns everything to silver.

SERGEI ESENIN, *USSR*

Aunt Sue's stories

Aunt Sue has a head full of stories
Aunt Sue has a whole heart full of stories.
Summer nights on the front porch
Aunt Sue cuddles a brown-faced child to her bosom
And tells him stories.

Black slaves
Working in the hot sun,
And black slaves
Walking in the dewy night,
And black slaves
Singing sorrow songs on the banks of a mighty river
Mingle themselves softly
In the flow of Old Aunt Sue's voice,
Mingle themselves softly
In the dark shadows that cross and re-cross
Aunt Sue's stories.

And the dark-faced child listening
Knows that Aunt Sue's stories are real stories.
He knows that Aunt Sue never got her stories
Out of any book at all,
But that they came
Right out of her own life.

The dark-faced child is quiet
On a Summer night
Listening to Aunt Sue's stories.

LANGSTON HUGHES, *USA*

Blowing bubbles

And this one goes to the lady next door
And this one goes to Mummy washing dishes.
This one goes to the church upon the hill
And this one to the pond and all its fishes.

This one drifts to the worms in the lawn
And this one to the birds in the trees.
This one will go to the shops up the road
And this one will go overseas.

I'm sending my bubbles all over the world
Watching as the wind makes them soar.
Some of them might get to countries far away,
But most seem to go next door.

KAY TOMS, *England*

Hill rolling

I kind of exploded inside,
and joy shot out of me.
I began to roll down the grassy hill.
I bent my knees up small, took a deep breath
and I was off.
My arms shot out sideways.
I gathered speed.
My eyes squinted
Sky and grass, dazzle and dark.

I went on forever,
My arms were covered with dents,
holes, squashed grass.
Before I knew it I was at the bottom.
The game was over.
The door of the classroom closed behind me.
I can smell chalk dust, and hear the voice of teacher,
to make me forget my hill.

ANDREW TAYLOR (10), *England*

18

The playground

In the playground
At the back of our house
There have been some changes.

They said the climbing frame was
NOT SAFE
So they sawed it down.

They said the paddling pool was
NOT SAFE
So they drained it dry.

They said the see-saw was
NOT SAFE
So they took it away.

They said the sandpit was
NOT SAFE
So they fenced it in.

They said the playground was
NOT SAFE
So they locked it up.

Sawn down
Drained dry
Taken away
Fenced in
Locked up

How do you feel?
Safe?

MICHAEL ROSEN,
    England

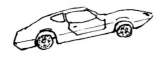

Boys will be boys

Boys will be boys, it's a fact of human nature,
And girls will grow up to be mothers.

Look at little Peter. Isn't he a terror?
Shooting all the neighbours with his cowboy gun.
Screaming like a jet-plane, always throwing something,
I just can't control him. Trouble – he's the one.

Ah but boys will be boys, it's a fact of human nature,
And girls will grow up to be mothers.

Look at little Janie. Doesn't she look pretty?
Playing with her dolly, proper little mum.
Never getting dirty, never being naughty –
Don't punch your sister, Peter. Now look what you've done.

Ah but boys will be boys, it's a fact of human nature,
And girls will grow up to be mothers.

What's come over Janie? Janie's turning nasty,
Left hook to the body, right hook to the eye.
Vicious little hussy! Now Peter's starting bawling.
What a bloody cissy! Who said you could cry?

Because boys will be boys, it's a fact of human nature,
And girls will grow up to be mothers.

Now things are topsy-turvy. Janie wants a football.
Peter just seems happy pushing prams along.
Makes you feel so guilty. Kids are such a worry.
Doctor, doctor, tell me, where did we go wrong?

Because boys must be boys, it's a fact of human nature,
And girls must grow up to be mothers.

LEON ROSSELSON, *England*

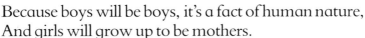

Lizzie

When we went over the park
Sunday mornings
We picked up sides.

Lizzie was our centre-forward
Because she had the best shot.

When the teachers
Chose the school team
Marshie was our centre-forward.

Lizzie wasn't allowed to play,
They said.

So she watched us lose, instead …

MICHAEL ROSEN, *England*

21

The quarrel

It was a joint partnership,
They owned this bike,
And they argued over it,
'I should have it, right?'

'It's my turn,' shouted Tom,
'Didn't you have it last night?'
'No, you had it.'
Then the quarrel turned into a fight.

One night over by the disco,
Down near County Hall,
They had one almighty battle,
And both ended up in hospital.

The bike had stood
In Joe's old shed next door,
And until the argument was over
It was used no more.

This went on
For a year and a day,
And when they next looked at the bike,
It had rusted away.

So no more did they argue,
They just sat on the wood,
And stared at the place
Where their bike once stood.

MARK WINYARD (11), *England*

Not enough

He gazed into the sweetstuff shops
This curly-headed boy,
The candy bars and lollipops
Lit up his face with joy.
The sherbert dabs and chocolate cream
Seemed near and yet so far,
With gums and bulls-eyes in between
All stacked up in a jar.
Reluctantly he turned away,
He could not have the stuff,
But maybe by next Saturday
His funds would be enough.
The boy seemed quite downcast and sad
But as he neared the school –
He threw the halfpence that he had
Over a garden wall.

STEPHEN HICKS, *England*

23

The plum tree

In the yard stands a small plum tree
Though you'd hardly believe it was one.
It has a railing round it
So no-one can knock it over.

It can't grow any bigger
Though that's what it wants to do.
That's out of the question –
It gets too little sun.

You'd hardly believe it was a plum tree
For it never bears a plum
But it is a plum tree
You can tell by the leaves.

BERTOLD BRECHT, *Germany*

The tramp tree

The tree with braces hanging out
Like rags of a tramp.
When the tree sways in the wind
It's like a tramp's arms with hairs on.
Their fingers at the top of the tree,
Their tearing fingers,
Tearing holes in the sky,
Trying to grab what isn't there
Trying to get free.
Spiky grass is his hair
And half his head is under the grass
With his brain as dirt
The roots are like veins
Pulled out with the strength of his arms
His body with worms all wriggling about
Keeping him down
The stones that he eats
Fall down his throat
And stop at an end.

ANTHONY BARTON (9), *England*

25

Red ant

Red ant, you are clinging to the bunch of cola nuts.
Red ant, you are clinging to the bunch of cola nuts.
You are not going to pluck it
Either to eat or to sell,
So what is the red ant going to do
With the bunch of cola nuts?

ANONYMOUS, *Ghana*

Mango, little mango

The mango stands for Africa
in its taste
in its smell
in its colour
in its shape.

The mango has the shape of a heart —
Africa too!
It has a taste that's hot, strong and sweet —
Africa too!
It has a reddy-brown shade
like the tanned plains
of my beloved earth.
Because of this I love you and your taste
Mango!
Heart of fruit, sweet and mild.

You are the love of Africa
because beating in your breast
is Africa's heart,
Oh mango, little mango,
love of Africa!

ANONYMOUS, *São Tomé and Principe*
Translated by Chris Searle

27

The catkin

Walking up the branch
Of the long
Pussy willow tree
Go the catkins
To settle in one place
Like cats' paws
Close to the stem
And all of a sudden they flower
Yellow bitty pollen
Blows around
A yellow mist
A dusty spray of soft gentle powder
In a yellow
Puddle.

LINDSAY HOLLEY (8), *England*

Little trotty wagtail

Little trotty wagtail, he went in the rain,
And tittering, tottering sideways he ne'er got straight again,
He stooped to get a worm, and looked up to catch a fly,
And then he flew away ere his feathers they were dry.

Little trotty wagtail, he waddled in the mud,
And left his little footmarks, trample where he would.
He waddled in the water-pudge and waggle went his tail,
And chirrupt up his wings to dry upon the garden rail.

Little trotty wagtail, you nimble all about,
And in the dimpling water-pudge you waddle in and out;
Your home is nigh at hand and in the warm pigsty,
So, little Master Wagtail, I'll bid you a good-bye.

JOHN CLARE, *England*

Bird song

The great gull hovers
on wings spread wide
above us, above us.
He stares, I shout!
His head is white,
his beak gapes,
his small round eyes
look far, look sharp!
      Qutiuk! Qutiuk!

The great skua hovers
on wings spread wide
above us, above us.
He stares, I shout!
His head is black,
his beak gapes,
his small round eyes
look far, look sharp!
      Ijoq! Ijoq!

The great raven hovers
on wings spread wide
above us, above us.
He stares, I shout!
His head is blue–black,
his beak is sharp
(does it have teeth?)
his eyes squint!
　　Qara! Qara!

And then there is the owl,
the great owl!
He hovers
on wings spread wide
above us, above us.
He stares, I shout!
His head is swollen,
his beak is hooked,
and his round eyes
have lids turned inside out,
red and heavy!
　　Oroq! Oroq!

TATILGAK, *Canada*

31

My house

My house is not my house
If there's someone without a house
Alongside my house.

The thing is that my house
can't be my house
if it's not also the house
of whoever has no house.

ANONYMOUS, *Cuba*

Family

There is only one man in the world
and his name is All Men.
There is only one woman in the world
and her name is All Women.
There is only one child in the world
and the child's name is All Children.

CARL SANDBURG, *USA*

My grandfather in Cyprus

I'd like to meet my grandad
But he lives in a land far away,
Where it is hot and sunny.
I hear he is an old man now,
His face is wrinkled like a lemon in the sun.
When we meet
We will talk in Greek,
Someday.

MICHAEL XENOFONTOS (11), *England*

Trouble in my flats

I live in a flat
where there's always trouble.
On the first floor
there's big fights brewing up.
On the second floor
there's graffiti on the walls.
On the third floor
the trouble-makers hang about.
On the fourth floor
the vandals are always seen.
On the fifth floor
there's always moaners moaning.
On the sixth floor
there's tramps asleep in the corridors.
But on the seventh floor
where I live
The atmosphere is nice and friendly
and do you know why?
Because the vandals and trouble-makers
    can't be bothered to walk seven floors.

DAVID OWOLABI (11), *England*

34

My brother Bob

My brother Bob
He's got no job,
He just hangs about
With his life hanging out.

ANONYMOUS, *England*

35

My noisy brother

My noisy brother's always noisy,
Going to bed, watching TV,
Waking up in the morning, always noisy.

My noisy brother is noisy at dinner,
He shouts GOODBYE loudly when going to secondary school,
He shouts like an elephant for fish and chips.

At night when my brother goes to sleep
He snores like my 40-year-old dad,
And when he wakes up in the morning·
He yells like mad for his breakfast,
But he's just my noisy brother.

My brother Muntaquim is not noisy at school,
But when he comes home the bombardment starts
Like a stool throwing.
He's the noisiest brother I ever had,
But he's still my noisy brother.

KASHIM CHOWDHURY (11), *England*

I can hear the trees whispering
the cats purring
the dogs barking
No wonder I can't get to sleep.

I can hear my dad in a rage
tearing up a page into little bits
while my mother sits crying
No wonder I can't get to sleep.

MARSHA PROVIDENCE, *England*

Hearing the cry of the cock

You're only an ordinary animal,
But every morning
Your cry brings in the day.
Cry of the cock!
You wake the people from sleep.
There's no doubt about it –
Your work is important!

HO CHI MINH, *Vietnam*

The shearer's wife

Before the glare o' dawn I rise
To milk the sleepy cows, an' shake
The droving dust from tired eyes,
Look about the rabbit traps, then bake
The children's bread.
There's hay to stook, an' beans to hoe,
An' ferns to cut in the scrub below.
Women must work, when men must go
Shearing from shed to shed.

I patch and darn, now evening comes,
An' tired I am with labour sore,
Tired o' the bush, the cows, the gums,
Tired, but we must dree[1] for long months more
What no tongue tells.
The moon is lonely in the sky,
Lonely is the bush, an' lonely I
Stare down the track, no horse draws nigh,
An' start … at the cattle bells.

LOUIS ESSON. *Australia*

1. Endure

The factory worker

This ordinary woman
Works in a factory up the road,
Putting bolts in the drill.
She presses the pedal that starts the drill working,
All day long from nine till four
Pressing the pedal that starts the drill working.
The dashing and the grinding,
The clicking and the shuttling
Are soothing to her ears,
Filling her arms with rhythm,
Her head with daydreams.
The siren sounds
And my mother faces the world again.

ANTHONY PARKER (11), *England*

Poverty knock

Poverty, poverty knock! Me loom is a-saying all day.
Poverty, poverty knock! Gaffer's too skinny to pay.
Poverty, poverty knock! Keepin' one eye on the clock.
Ah know ah can guttle[1], when ah hear me shuttle
Go: poverty, poverty knock!

Up every mornin' at five.
Ah wonder that we keep alive.
Tired an' yawnin' on the cold mornin'
It's back to the dreary old drive.

Oh dear, we're goin' to be late.
Gaffer is stood at the gate
We're out o' pocket, our wages they're docket;
We'll 'a' to buy grub on the slate.

An' when our wages they'll bring,
We're often short of a string[2]
While we are fratchin'[3] wi' gaffer for snatchin'
We know to his brass he will cling.

We've got to wet our own yarn
By dippin' it into the tarn[4].
It's wet an' soggy an' makes us feel groggy,
An' there's mice in that dirty old barn.

Oh dear, me poor 'ead it sings.
Ah should have woven three strings,
But threads are breakin' and my back is achin'
Oh dear, ah wish ah had wings.

ANONYMOUS, *England*

1. Eat
2. Length of cloth
3. Quarrelling
4. Water

Awo! (Thank you!)

Women who never have to hoe, awo!
Give me a hoe that doesn't dig, awo!
They have tied a handle to the blade, awo!
Tied it tightly just the wrong way, awo!
Let me clear the field, awo!
Dig, let me dig, let me dig! Awo!
And I will have fat meat, awo!
Now just let me weed, awo!
Let me try to walk, awo!
My back is killing me, awo!

ANONYMOUS, *Uganda*

Guinea corn

Guinea corn, I long to see you
Guinea corn, I long to plant you
Guinea corn, I long to mould you
Guinea corn, I long to weed you
Guinea corn, I long to hoe you
Guinea corn, I long to top you
Guinea corn, I long to cut you
Guinea corn, I long to dry you
Guinea corn, I long to beat you
Guinea corn, I long to trash you
Guinea corn, I long to parch you
Guinea corn, I long to grind you
Guinea corn, I long to turn you
Guinea corn, I long to eat you

ANONYMOUS, *Jamaica*

The coals burner

Chop!
Chop!
Chop!
Chopping away,
Arms in full sway,
All the day.

Pull!
Pull!
Pull!
Pulling along,
As to a song
All day long.

Tumble!
Fumble!
Grumble!
At the fall
Of the logs,
In the sun or fog.

Chop!
Chop!
Pack!
Pack!
Close together,
Saving bother.

Dig!
Dig!
Digging away,
That's the way,
He'll be gay
On his pay day.

Covering!
Catching!
Viewing!
Fumes,
Smoke and flames,
Waiting for his gain.

Drawing!
Collecting!
Bagging!
Transporting
To the market,
For cash in his pocket.

RENALPH GEBON,
Grenada

Doon the pit

Aa've seen young lads gan doon the Pit
  inside the dorty cage,
T'woork beneath the green, green grass
  t'orn a livin' wage;
And they were strite as strite can be,
  with cheeks a rosy hue,
Aa've seen the same lads come t'Bank
  aall bent and black and blue.

NORMAN THOMPSON, *England*

Hunger

Fear hung over me.
I dared not try
to hold out in my hut.

Hungry and chilled,
I stumbled inland,
tripping, falling constantly.

At Little Musk Ox Lake
the trout made fun of me;
they wouldn't bite.

On I crawled,
and reached the Young Man's River
where I had caught salmon once.

I prayed
for fish or reindeer
swimming in the lake.

My thought
reeled into nothingness
like run-out fishing line.

ANONYMOUS ESKIMO SONG, *Canada*

The plough

I clench my fist
and bury the plough in the earth.
For years and years I have worked
no wonder I am worn out.

Butterflies are flying,
crickets are singing,
my skin gets darker and darker
and the sun glares, glares and glares.
Sweat furrows me,
I make furrows in the earth
on and on.

I hold fast to hope
when I think of my other star.
'It is never too late,' she tells me,
'The dove will fly one day.'

Butterflies are flying,
crickets are singing,
my skin gets darker and darker
and the sun glares, glares and glares.
And in the evening going home
in the sky I see a star.
'It is never too late,' she tells me,
'The dove will fly one day.'
As tight as a yoke
my fist is full of hope
because everything will change.

VICTOR JARA, *Chile*

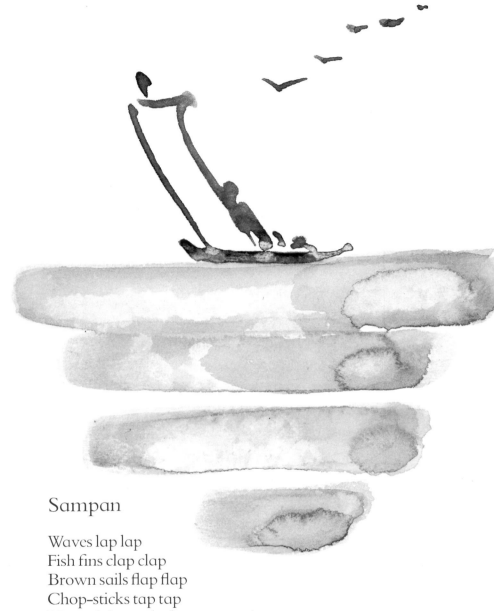

Sampan

Waves lap lap
Fish fins clap clap
Brown sails flap flap
Chop-sticks tap tap
Up and down the long green river
Ohe Ohe lanterns quiver
Willow branches brush the river
Ohe Ohe lanterns quiver
Waves lap lap
Fish fins clap clap
Brown sails flap flap
Chop-sticks tap tap

TAO LANG PEE, *China*

Children cry

Children cry for all reasons,
For no reason at all,
At no sign of danger,
Playing games with a ball.

Children cry out of mischief,
Many a child will cry
Prompted by childish cunning
For a star in the sky.

But when in grim earnest
Cruel enemies strike
Children, no matter how different,
In all lands cry alike.

VASILI FYODOROV, *USSR*

The wheel around the world

If all the world's children
wanted to play holding hands
they could happily make
a wheel around the sea.

If all the world's children
wanted to play holding hands
they could be sailors
and build a bridge across the seas.

What a beautiful chorus we would make
singing around the earth
if all the humans in the world
wanted to dance holding hands!

CHILDREN'S SONG, *Mozambique*
Translated by Chris Searle

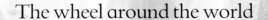

Jamaica market

Honey, pepper, leaf-green limes,
Pagan fruit whose names are rhymes,
Mangoes, breadfruit, ginger-roots,
Granadillas, bamboo-shoots,
Cho-cho, ackees, tangerines,
Lemons, purple Congo-beans,
Sugar, okras, kola-nuts,
Citrons, hairy coconuts,
Fish, tobacco, native hats,
Gold bananas, woven mats,
Plantains, wild-thyme, pallid leeks,
Pigeons with their scarlet beaks,
Oranges and saffron yams,
Baskets, ruby guava jams,
Turtles, goat-skins, cinnamon,
Allspice, conch-shells, golden rum.
Black skins, babel – and the sun
That burns all colours into one.

AGNES MAXWELL-HALL, *Jamaica*

The dying British sergeant

Come all you good people, where'er you be,
Who walk on the land or sail by the sea,
Come listen to the words of a dyin' man,
I think you will remember them.

'Twas in October, the eighteenth day,
Our ship set sail for Amerikay,
The drums and the trumpets loud did sound,
And then to Boston we were bound.

And when to Boston we did come
We thought by the aid of our British guns
To make them Yankees own our king,
And daily tribute to him bring.

But to our sad and sore surprise
We saw men like grasshoppers rise,
'Freedom or death!' was all their cry,
Indeed they were not feared to die.

When I received my deathly wound
I bid farewell to England's ground,
My wife and children shall mourn for me
Whilst I lie dead in Amerikee.

ANONYMOUS, USA

Johnny I hardly knew you

With your guns and drums and drums and guns
The enemy nearly slew you,
Oh my darlin' dear, you look so queer,
Och, Johnny I hardly knew you.

Where are your eyes that were so mild
When my heart you so beguiled?
Why did you run from me and the child?
Och, Johnny I hardly knew you.

Where are your legs that used to run
When you went for to carry a gun?
Indeed your dancin' days are done,
Och, Johnny I hardly knew you.

I'm happy for to see you home,
Oh my darlin', so pale and wan,
So low in flesh, so high in bone,
Och, Johnny I hardly knew you.

They're rolling out the guns again
But they never will take our sons again,
No, they never will take our sons again,
Johnny, I'm swearin' to you.

ANONYMOUS, *Ireland*

53

Road of peace

Build a road of peace before us,
Build it wide and deep and long.
Speed the slow and check the eager
Help the weak and curb the strong.
None shall push beside another
None shall let another fall,
March together sister, brother,
All for one
And one for all!

PAUL ROBESON, *USA*

One tree

one tree
so many leaves
one tree

one river
so many creeks
all are going to one sea

one head
so many thoughts
thoughts among which one good one
must be

one god
so many ways of worshipping
but one father

one Suriname
so many hair types
so many skin colours
so many tongues
one people

DOBRU RAVALES,
Suriname

I LIVE IN THE CITY

I live in the city, yes I do,
I live in the city, yes I do,
I live in the city, yes I do,
Made by human hands.

Black hands, white hands, yellow and brown
All together built this town,
Black hands, white hands, yellow and brown
All together make the wheels go round.

Black hands, brown hands, yellow and white
Built the buildings tall and bright,
Black hands, brown hands, yellow and white
Filled them all with shining light.

Black hands, white hands, brown and tan
Milled the flour and cleaned the pan,
Black hands, white hands, brown and tan –
The working woman and the working man.

I live in the city, yes I do,
I live in the city, yes I do,
I live in the city, yes I do,
Made by human hands.

ANONYMOUS, *USA*

Old woman's song

Shall I tell you who is weak?
The weak buy men for riches
And sell them for famine,
They paint flowers in the desert and call it a garden,
They smile like the torturer and bow like the judge,
They lead armies to hell so that they shall have a kingdom to rule in.

Shall I tell you who is strong?
Child, you are strong,
You have nothing and your hands are small
But the world spins like clay on a potter's wheel
And you will shape it with your hands.

EDWARD BOND, *England*

Index of first lines and titles

Index of countries and poets

Acknowledgements

Acknowledgements

We are indebted to the following poets and publishers for permission to reproduce copyright material:

Allison and Busby for 'Bird song' translated by Tom Lowenstein from *Eskimo Poems*.

Keith Armstrong for 'Doon the pit' by Norman Thompson.

Carcanet Press for 'Night' by Sergei Esenin translated by Geoffrey Thurley from *Confessions of a Hooligan*.

Centerprise Publishing Project for 'Blowing bubbles' by Kay Toms.

Daily Mirror Children's Literary Competition (1974) for 'The catkin' by Lindsay Holley.

Humanities Team, Daneford School, London for 'My grandfather in Cyprus' by Michael Xenofontos, 'My noisy brother' by Kashim Chowdhury and 'Trouble in my flats' by David Owolabi.

Journeyman Press for 'Boys will be boys' by Leon Rosselson.

Methuen London for 'Old woman's song' by Edward Bond from *We Come to the River*.

Mighty Oak Music Ltd for 'The plough' (English translation of 'Elarado') by Victor Jara from *Victor Jara: His Life and Songs*.

Museum of Modern Art for 'Family.' From the prologue by Carl Sandburg to *The Family of Man*. Copyright © 1955 The Museum of Modern Art, New York. All rights reserved.

National Book League for 'The tramp tree' by Anthony Barton and 'The factory worker' by Anthony Parker from *Children's Words 1971*.

Random House Inc for 'Aunt Sue's stories' by Langston Hughes from *Selected Poems of Langston Hughes*.

Chris Searle for 'Mango, little mango', 'Not enough' by Stephen Hicks and 'The wheel around the world'.

Andrew Taylor for 'Hill rolling'.

Writers and Readers Publishing Co-op for 'The plum tree' by Bertold Brecht from *Politics of Literacy*.

The following poems are used by permission of the author and appear for the first time in this anthology unless otherwise stated:

'Lizzie' and 'The playground' by Michael Rosen.

'My brother Bob' by Chris Searle.

'Shout' by Keith Armstrong from *Giving Blood*, People's Publications, Newcastle upon Tyne.

'The coals burner' by Renalph Gebon.

While every effort has been made to trace the owners of copyrights in a few cases this has proved impossible and we take this opportunity of tendering our apologies to any owners whose rights may have been unwittingly infringed.

PRINTED IN BELGIUM BY

INTERNATIONAL BOOK PRODUCTION